Did Y...

TORBA...
SOUTH HAMS

A MISCELLANY

Compiled by Julia Skinner

With particular reference to the work of John Bainbridge,
Martin Dunning, Dennis Needham and Peggy Parnell

THE FRANCIS FRITH COLLECTION

www.francisfrith.com

First published in the United Kingdom in 2013 by The Francis Frith Collection®

This edition published exclusively for Bradwell Books in 2013
For trade enquiries see: www.bradwellbooks.com or tel: 0800 834 920
ISBN 978-1-84589-735-2

Text and Design copyright The Francis Frith Collection®
Photographs copyright The Francis Frith Collection® except where indicated.

British Library Cataloguing in Publication Data

Did You Know? Torbay and The South Hams - A Miscellany
Compiled by Julia Skinner
With particular reference to the work of John Bainbridge, Martin Dunning, Dennis Needham and
Peggy Parnell

The Francis Frith Collection
6 Oakley Business Park,
Wylye Road, Dinton,
Wiltshire SP3 5EU
Tel: +44 (0) 1722 716 376
Email: info@francisfrith.co.uk
www.francisfrith.com

Printed and bound in Malaysia
Contains material sourced from responsibly managed forests

Front Cover: **COCKINGTON, THE VILLAGE 1912** 64687ap
Frontispiece: **NEWTON FERRERS, THE RIVER YEALM 1924** 76037
Contents: **YEALMPTON, 'OLD MOTHER HUBBARD'S COTTAGE', MARKET STREET c1950**
Y9001

The colour-tinting is for illustrative purposes only, and is not intended to be historically accurate

CONTENTS

INTRODUCTION

The great sweep of Torbay runs from the promontory of Hope's Nose, near Torquay, to its southernmost point of Berry Head, east of Brixham. Its coastline boasts twenty different beaches and three major resorts, Torquay, Paignton and Brixham, all very different from each other in character. Originally a small fishing hamlet, Torquay first attracted convalescent visitors, drawn there by its mild climate; then the fledgling resort acquired a certain cachet in the early 19th century when the Napoleonic wars prevented people from travelling abroad, and they discovered the delights of Torbay instead. The extent and form of Torquay was established in those long-ago days, when it was famous for its style and sophistication and known as 'the Queen of Watering Places'. Renowned for its Mediterranean-like setting, Torquay now rejoices in its newer designation as 'The Queen of the English Riviera'. Paignton is a happy family resort, with two miles of safe bathing on golden sandy beaches. Brixham, in contrast, is a charming old fishing town in a rugged and romantic setting, beloved of artists, photographers and the tourists who throng the quay in the summer to watch the trawlers come and go.

TORQUAY, WALDON HILL 1912 64663

SOUTH POOL, THE CREEK FROM GULLET 1922 73254

The South Hams is an area with a very particular identity. It stretches from Torbay in the east to Plymouth in the west, with Dartmoor to the north and the sea to the south. This is a region of ancient towns, picturesque villages and spectacular coastal scenery, as well as some of the loveliest pastoral countryside in England, a patchwork of fields set on a wrinkled, folded landscape with thick woodlands in the valleys and isolated copses capping the higher hills. The 'Ham' of its name is an old word meaning 'a sheltered place', and the mild climate enjoyed by this region makes it an area of fertile agricultural farmland, drawing its nourishment from rich red soils. The bleak hills of Dartmoor on the northern edge of the South Hams are responsible in no short measure for the landscape of the region. The high plateau of the moor receives 70-80 inches of rain annually, and over the millennia all that water rushing down off Dartmoor has carved deep, snaking river valleys; when the sea level rose at the end of the last Ice Age these valleys became flooded far inland from the river mouths, giving rise to the beautiful tidal estuaries (correctly known as rias) with their mudflats and creeks that are such a feature of the coastal area.

DEVON DIALECT WORDS & PHRASES

'Bloin' a (h)ooley' – very windy.

'You gert lummock' – you great fool.

'Mitching' – playing truant.

'Right maid?' and **'Right boy?'** – a standard greeting to men and women of any age.

'Over the way' – over there.

'Dimpsy' – twilight.

'Teddies' – potatoes.

'Likkies' – leeks.

'Maze' or **mazed'** – mad or daft.

'Cakey' – silly.

'Goosegogs' – gooseberries.

'Chuffy pigs' – woodlice.

'Skimmish' – squeamish.

'Grockle' – a holidaymaker.

'Smeeching' – smoking, such as when wet wood is put on a fire.

'Smeech mark' – a smudge or smoky mark.

'What be telling of?' – 'What are you talking about?

'Lants' – **sand eels,** and **'going lanting'** – going to catch sand eels.

'Vor on!' – go faster, or get going.

'Proper' – really or very, as in **'ee's proper 'ansome'** – 'he's very handsome'; also used to mean very good, as in **'proper job'** for something well done.

'Dryth' – good warm, breezy weather for drying clothes on washday, as in **'There's a good dryth'.** Also used for the opposite, as in **'There's no dryth in the air today!'**

HAUNTED TORBAY & THE SOUTH HAMS

Overlooking Torquay's harbour is St John's Church, which is reputed to be haunted by the ghosts of two former organists who were seen and heard playing music in the church after their respective deaths in 1883 and 1953; there have also been reports that organists playing there have sometimes felt that an unseen force was guiding their fingers.

Near Totnes is the picturesque shell of Berry Pomeroy Castle, the home of the Pomeroy family until the 1540s, when it was sold to Edward Seymour (c1500-1552), 1st Duke of Somerset. Subsequently five generations of Seymours lived there, and built a grand four-storey mansion within the medieval castle walls. The castle fell into disrepair after the Civil War and by 1700 had been abandoned to fall into ruin. A number of ghosts are said to roam the castle, including the Blue Lady who tries to lure you up to a tower by apparently beckoning for help – but if you go to her, you will fall to your death from the castle walls. Legend says that in her earthly life she was a daughter of a lord of the castle who sired a child on her, but when the baby was born she murdered it because of its parentage; now her bitter, revengeful spirit cannot rest and wanders the castle mourning its loss. Another of the castle's ghosts is the White Lady, the unhappy spirit of Lady Margaret Pomeroy who was imprisoned in a dungeon there by her jealous elder sister Eleanor because of a dispute over a love rival, and left to starve to death.

In past times the Pilchard Inn on Burgh Island, offshore from Bigbury-on-Sea, was a favourite haunt of the smuggler Tom Crocker – and it still is, according to the local tale that Crocker still wanders the pub in spirit form, especially around 14th August, the anniversary of the day he was shot and killed there, when he rattles door handles and generally causes mischief around the pub.

TORBAY & THE SOUTH HAMS MISCELLANY

The first part of Torquay's name comes from Tor Hill, the rocky outcrop above the village of Torre that preceded the modern town. The 'quay' part refers to the landing stage built by the Premonstratensian canons of Torre Abbey, who controlled the fishing rights in Torbay in the Middle Ages. Torre Abbey was closed in 1539 by King Henry VIII. Some of its buildings were demolished, whilst others were transformed by the Cary family into a fine country house that now houses a museum and art gallery. Artworks there include the contents of the studio of the prominent Victorian sculptor Frederick Thrupp, the largest surviving collection from a Victorian sculptor's studio in the UK.

Torquay's main beach, Torre Abbey Sands, has the best sand for making sandcastles – and that's official! In 2004, scientists from Bournemouth University announced they had travelled all round Britain's coast collecting samples of beach sand to judge which was best for sandcastle construction, using the optimum sand and water combination of one part water to eight parts of sand. They declared that Torquay's extremely fine-grained sand with its excellent cohesive powers was the best in Britain for the job!

In Torquay's early years as a seaside resort many of its visitors were invalids, who came there because of the mild climate and clean air of the area. The town's motto is 'Salus at Facilitas', meaning 'Health and Happiness' a reminder of its early role as a health resort as well as its continuing popularity as a place for family holidays.

Torbay's famous palm trees first arrived in the 1820s and flourish all along the coast because of the mild, sheltered climate and well-drained soil of the area. Although they are known as 'Torbay palms', the trees originate from New Zealand, botanical name Cordyline australis, where they are also known as 'cabbage trees' because of their edible young shoots. Cordyline australis used to be classified as a species of lily, hence its alternative name of 'Lily Palm', but scientists have now re-categorised it as a member of the asparagus family.

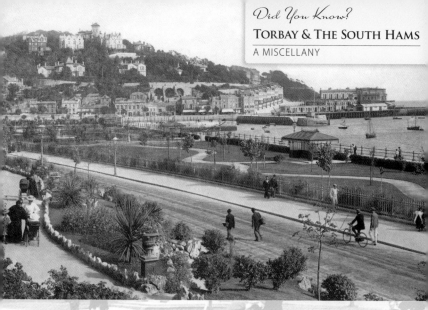

TORQUAY, VANE HILL, THE ROCK WALK AND PRINCESS GARDENS
1896 38593a

Above Torquay's harbour stands Vane Hill, named after a prominent weather-vane that stood there in the early 19th century. The building with a tower seen on its summit in this view is the Villa Lugano (now subdivided into three properties), which was built as a copy of a building on the shore of Italy's Lake Lugano. It was constructed in 1872, reputedly for the first American Ambassador to be based in England.

During the Second World War Torquay was an embarkation point for American troops for the Normandy landings on D-Day, 6th June 1944. On the north side of the harbour, at Beacon Quay, you can still see two broad concrete slipways leading into the water that were built for the embarkation of troops from the 4th US Infantry Division onto LCTs (Landing Craft Troop) on 5th June 1944, bound for 'Utah Beach'. The slipways were built in 1943 by British Royal Engineers who later financed the building of the nearby D-Day Embarkation Ramps memorial wall. They are possibly the best-surviving examples of D-Day fabric in the country, and are now Grade 2 listed historic monuments.

This view shows the beautiful Pavilion at
Torquay in the year it opened as a 'Palace
of Pleasure', catering for all styles of
popular and classical entertainment –
the building is now used as a shopping
centre. It was after a concert at the
Pavilion in 1913 that Archie Christie
proposed to local girl Agatha Miller,
who went on to become world famous
after their marriage as the crime novelist
Agatha Christie. A bronze bust of the
'Queen of Crime' now stands in the small
garden opposite the Pavilion.

TORQUAY, THE PAVILION 1912 64671

TORQUAY, THE STRAND AND CLOCK TOWER 1920 69586

Agatha Christie was born Agatha Miller in 1890 in a now demolished house called Ashfield in Barton Road at Torquay, and grew up in the town. She married Archie Christie in 1914 and the couple spent their honeymoon at the Grand Hotel in Torquay. During the First World War she worked as a member of the VAD (Voluntary Aid Detachment) in a makeshift hospital in the Public Hall attached to Torquay's Town Hall in Castle Circus, first nursing wounded soldiers and then working in the pharmacy, where she gained a considerable knowledge of poisons that she later used to great effect in her books. It was also during the war that, in 1915, she noticed a small Belgian man on a tram in Torquay, one of many refugees from the conflict who had come to the town from Belgium; she used him as the model for one of her most famous fictional creations, the Belgian detective Hercule Poirot, who appeared in her first published novel, 'The Mysterious Affair at Styles', written in 1916.

Until the 1840s Paignton was a small agricultural and fishing settlement half a mile inland. In the mid 19th century it became popular with convalescents, and its beach – longer and better than Torquay's – began to attract holidaymakers, but it was the arrival of the railway in 1859 that triggered its development as Torbay's family seaside resort. Numerous hotels and villas were constructed as the resort grew and expanded to cope with the subsequent influx of tourists, eventually engulfing the neighbouring settlements of Goodrington and Preston. One of the most important entrepreneurs to arrive in the town at this time was Arthur Hyde Dendy, whose contribution to Paignton is recalled in the names of Dendy Road and Hyde Road. Amongst many other things, it was Dendy who established two of the most essential requirements of a successful Victorian seaside resort, bathing machines on the beach and a pier where visitors could promenade. Dendy originally purchased Teignmouth's pier for the town, planning to have it reconstructed at Paignton, but structural difficulties prevented this so he commissioned a brand new pier for Paignton, which opened in 1879.

PAIGNTON, BATHING MACHINES ON THE BEACH 1896 38545x

PAIGNTON, CHURCH STREET 1912 64719

The oldest part of Paignton is around Winner Street (its name derives from the vineyard that was there in the Middle Ages) and Church Street, near St John's Church. Amongst many items of interest in the church are a gruesome tomb with a carving of a decaying corpse on top, a type known as a 'cadaver' monument, and the fine chantry chapel of the Kirkhams, a prominent local family of the past; it was built by Nicholas Kirkham (1434-1516), whose effigy is probably one of the recumbent figures on the tombs. Although much damaged, the decoratively-carved screen of white Beer stone that separates the chantry from the nave is one of the finest examples of its type in the country.

A nickname for Paignton people in the past was 'flat poles', because of the 'very large and superior' flat pole cabbages that were grown in the area, according to John Marius Wilson's 'Imperial Gazetteer of England and Wales' of 1870-72. Huge quantities of cabbages were grown around the town until the late 19th century, and were shipped out from Paignton's harbour to the markets of London as well as for export overseas.

PAIGNTON, OLDWAY c1955 P2010

The building that houses Barclays Bank in Palace Avenue in Paignton was once the home of the mathematician and scientist Oliver Heaviside (1850-1925), who lived above his brother's music shop there from 1889 to 1897. In his laboratory on the second floor he worked on electromagnetic theories that culminated in his prediction in 1902 of what is now called the Heaviside Layer of the ionosphere, a region of the upper atmosphere of Earth that forms an important part of atmospheric electricity, off which radio signals are reflected around the planet's curvature.

A famous building in Paignton is Oldway Mansion, off Torquay Road, originally the home of the millionaire Isaac Merritt Singer (1811-1875) of sewing machine fame, who came to Britain from New York for personal and business reasons and chose Paignton as the place to live. He started to build his mansion in the 1870s, but died before it was completed. In the early 1900s one of his sons, Paris Singer, took over the house and transformed it into the magnificent edifice that stands today, modelled on the Palace of Versailles. From 1909 until 1917, when they parted company, he lived there with his lover, the famous dancer Isadora Duncan.

At the southern end of Torbay is Brixham, which became known as 'the great fishery of the west' in the 19th century after its fishermen refined the art of deep-sea trawling, dragging nets along the seabed to catch fish near the seafloor. The boats used for this were the famous Brixham trawlers, two-masted yawls which for their size (about 75ft) were some of the most powerful sailing vessels of their day, noted for their speed and also for their red sails, which the fishermen coated with local red ochre to protect them from seawater. In the days of sail, trawling involved going to sea in severe weather so the wind could propel the boat fast enough to keep the net moving through the water without folding or snagging. Although this technique was hazardous it was also a profitable way to make a living. In the early 19th century, twelve Brixham fishermen used their profits to buy a one-fourth share in the Lordship of the Manor of Brixham. These shares have now been divided and sub-divided so much that most Brixham fishermen with a longstanding connection to the town might rightly be referred to as 'M'lord'.

BRIXHAM, TRAWLERS WAITING FOR A BREEZE 1889 21556

Above Brixham's harbour in the background of this view is All Saints' Church, which dates from the 1820s. Its first vicar was the much-loved Reverend Henry Francis Lyte (1793-1847), who is said to have walked across the harbour on the decks of the anchored fishing fleet, preaching to the fishermen before they set out to sea. Reverend Lyte lived for many years at Berry Head House on the cliffs above the town where he wrote a number of well-known hymns, including 'Abide with Me', which he penned whilst watching the sun set over Torbay shortly before he died, and which generations of Brixham fishermen have sung as a prayer whilst setting out to sea. The church was damaged in a storm in 1872 and was rebuilt, with the support of local fishing families, as a memorial to Reverend Lyte. A carillon of bells plays his hymn tunes throughout the day, and the sound of 'Abide with Me' echoes over the harbour in the evening.

BRIXHAM, THE HARBOUR c1939 B214022

14

Beside Brixham's harbour is the only statue in the country whose plinth bears an inscription in Dutch. (It translates as 'The Liberty of England, restored by Orange'.) The statue represents William, Prince of the Dutch state of Orange, and commemorates Brixham's part in a significant event in British history. On November 5th 1688 the Protestant William of Orange landed here with his forces after a group of influential Englishmen invited him to come and take the throne from his unpopular father-in-law, the Catholic King James II, and end his absolutionist monarchy. William's arrival was the beginning of the 'Glorious Revolution', so called because so little blood was spilt; four weeks later King James fled the country, and William and his wife Mary, James's daughter, became King William III and Queen Mary II.

After spending the night in Brixham the future King William moved north to Newton Abbot. On the way he stopped at a humble thatched cottage at Longcombe, south of Berry Pomeroy, where he held his first meeting, or parliament, with his supporters. The cottage (originally two adjoining dwellings) has been known as Parliament Cottage or Parliament House ever since. A commemorative stone in its front garden bears the inscription: 'William Prince of Orange is said to have held his first Parliament here in November 1688.'

When he landed at Brixham, William of Orange issued his famous declaration 'The liberties of England and the Protestant religion I will maintain'. This is recalled in Brixham Cricket Club's insignia of 'Je Meintiendray' – the medieval Dutch version of 'I will maintain'.

Brixham is sheltered from the wild channel gales by the towering cliffs of Berry Head, the most southerly point of Torbay. At its tip is the tiny Berry Head lighthouse station, which is the shortest lighthouse in the British Isles, at only 5 metres (16ft) tall, but also one of the highest, perched high on the cliffs of the headland at 58 metres (190ft) above mean sea level.

The five major rivers of the South Hams region all have their source on Dartmoor – the Dart, Avon, Erme, Yealm and Plym – and cut through the coastal plain every few miles, dividing the area into neat little packets. They all have their own character, and each has played its part in the history of the South Hams. Settlements grew up around fords over the rivers, for it was here that people crossed paths, made contacts and traded; eventually, when the hamlet or village had become busy and wealthy enough to warrant and afford it, a bridge was built. Thus the old tidal ford at Aveton Gifford was in time spanned by the bridge that today carries the A379, while at places such as Harbertonford the ford and bridge can be seen side by side. Other settlements became wealthy because of their position on the rivers, perhaps through fishing, trading through their ports, or using the water to power mills making products such as as woollen cloth and paper.

The most northerly village in the South Hams is Holne, west of Ashburton, where the eastern and northern boundaries of the parish are formed by the River Dart as it flows off Dartmoor. Wherever there is fast flowing water there is the danger of floods and drowning accidents, and it has long been said that once a year the River Dart demands a human life. An old saying goes 'Dart, Dart, cruel Dart, every year thou claim'st a heart', and Dartmoor folklore is that when the river is ready for 'a heart' it will 'cry' out and summon its victim. The Dart does indeed seem to 'cry' in certain weather conditions, and an eerie sound can often be heard coming from the river after a summer thunderstorm near the Brad Stones (marked 'Broadstone on the OS map) or on Bench Tor when a north-westerly wind is blowing – both places are north of the Venford reservoir, a short distance north of Holne.

As the Dart flows south it passes through Staverton, a few miles north of Totnes, where the seven-arched bridge that crosses the river dates from 1413 and is considered to be one of the best examples of medieval bridges surviving in Devon. Staverton Bridge has seen its fair share of incidents, especially in the form of floods, but perhaps the oddest incident on the bridge took place in 1436 when the vicar, Sir John Laa, killed John Gayne with a knife after an argument. The Bishop accepted that he had been provoked, and let him off!

Slate quarrying used to be an important industry in the Staverton area, from the Penn Ricca quarries which closed in 1908. The industry reached its height in the mid 19th century, when Penn Ricca slate was used on the roof of the Houses of Parliament in London.

STAVERTON, THE BRIDGE 1889 21643

Totnes is the lowest bridging point on the Dart, and the highest point to which ocean-going ships can sail. The town's position on the Dart ensured its prosperity as a centre of trade in the past, particularly in cloth. The ready power the river supplied and the softness of its water allowed the growth of a thriving woollen industry there, where locally produced wool was sheared, combed, carded, spun and eventually woven into robust Devon cloth. Reminders of the river's importance are found in several placenames around the town, such as Steamer Quay, Baltic Wharf (a reference to the timber trade with Scandinavia), and Fishcheaters' Lane, so called because it was used to avoid paying duty on the salmon which provided a living from the river for hundreds of years.

A merchant of Totnes who grew rich selling pilchards and dried eels in the 16th century was Nicholas Ball, whose house in the High Street now forms part of the local branch of Barclays Bank; after his death in 1586 his widow Anne married Sir Thomas Bodley, who used her wealth to found the Bodleian Library in Oxford.

TOTNES, THE LANDING PLACE AND THE BRIDGE 1896 38213

TOTNES, EAST GATE 1928 80999

Medieval Totnes was a walled town with four entrances, or gates. This view shows the East Gate, which has been rebuilt several times in its history. Near it on the left of this view is one of the finest Tudor townhouses in the country. It was built in the 1570s for a wealthy cloth merchant and now houses the Totnes Elizabethan House Museum.

One of the rooms in the Totnes Elizabethan House Museum is dedicated to the life and work of Charles Babbage (1791-1871), a mathematician, inventor and mechanical engineer who is credited with inventing the first mechanical programmable computer, which paved the way for more complex designs later. He had family connections with Totnes, where his grandfather Benjamin Babbage had been the mayor of the town in 1754. Babbage himself was born in London where his father was a banker, but he received some of his schooling at the King Edward VI Grammar School in Totnes after his family moved back to Devon in 1808.

Overlooking the Dart downriver from Totnes is Sharpham House, sited on the peninsula between the river and its tributary of Bow Creek. Sharpham House was designed in the 1760s by the notable architect Sir Robert Taylor, who incorporated an earlier building, and although there have been later additions and alterations it remains a fine example of English Palladian architecture. An impressive feature inside the house is Taylor's great oval stair hall, where a cantilevered Portland stone staircase seems to float up through three storeys through the centre of the building to a top-lit dome. Sir Robert Taylor was commissioned to design the house by Captain Philemon Pownoll, RN, of HMS 'Favourite', who decided to build a grand mansion with the prize money he received for capturing a Spanish treasure ship in 1762, during the Seven Years War. Captain Pownall was killed in action at sea in 1780 and there is a monument to him in the church at nearby Ashprington. If you are visiting this church, look out for the lovely carved pulpit and see if you can find the little snail attacking the vine leaves on its decoration!

SHARPHAM, SHARPHAM HOUSE AND THE BATHING HOUSE 1899
44587

HARBERTONFORD, GENERAL VIEW c1960 H494004

Bow Creek is where the River Harbourne joins the Dart after rising on Dartmoor and flowing through Harbourneford (where it passes under an ancient and picturesque 'clapper bridge'), Harberton and Harbertonford, before emptying into Bow Creek between Ashprington and Tuckenhay. Although the Harbourne valley now seems quiet and overgrown, this used to be an important place of industry. For many years the fast-flowing Harbourne provided water power for all kinds of mills, the largest of which was the woollen mill at Harbertonford, where at one time around a hundred people were employed. Water from the river drove four turbines working off the millpond (now filled in), which drove the mill's machines. The mill was famous for its serge cloth which was used mainly by the military for making thick blankets and hardy uniforms. The Harbertonford woollen mill closed in 1956 after operating for around 200 years, and is seen in this photograph shortly before its chimney was demolished a few years later.

Stoke Gabriel lies on a creek on the eastern side of the River Dart. In the village churchyard is a very ancient yew tree. According to an old rhyme, your wish will come true if you can walk backwards around the tree seven times without stumbling!

Further downriver on the eastern bank is Greenway House, which the crime novelist Agatha Christie and her second husband Max Malloran bought in 1938 and used as their holiday home until their deaths in the 1970s. It is now cared for by the National Trust. Greenway was commandeered for housing officers of the American armed forces during the Second World War, one of whom was Lieutenant Marshall of Flotilla 10 of the US Coastguard. In 1943 he painted a colourful frieze around the top of the wall in the library, depicting all the significant events of their war, starting at their base in Florida and ending with an image of an Infantry Landing Craft on the River Dart below Greenway. Agatha liked the frieze so much when she returned to the house after the war that she kept it as part of the room's decoration.

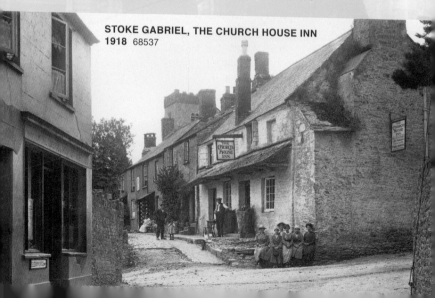

STOKE GABRIEL, THE CHURCH HOUSE INN
1918 68537

Moving downriver, on the western bank of the tidal reaches of the Dart is Dittisham, known as 'Ditsum' by locals. A short distance downstream from the main village is Vipers Quay, which until the 1960s was the site of an old gun battery, probably dating from the 16th or 17th century, that protected Totnes from hostile shipping going upriver. Out in the middle of the river off Vipers Quay is the Anchor Stone, which marked the northern limit of the deep water where big ships could be laid up. According to local legend, the Anchor Stone was also where any unfaithful, wayward or nagging wives from the village were tied as punishment, hence its other name of the Scold Stone.

Dittisham was once famous for its plum orchards, and particularly for a localised plum variety. The Dittisham Plum, also known as the Dittisham Small Red, only grows around this one village in Devon, and many cottage gardens in the area contain a Dittisham Plum tree. There are many theories about how the plum came to grow there, none of which can be substantiated: one is that the variety originated from a cargo of fruit or seedlings that was dumped by a ship's captain when he was unable to sell it, which the villagers found on the strand line and planted in their gardens; another is that the original trees were brought to the area by nuns from the nearby Priory of Cornworthy; and yet another is that the original plum trees came to the village from Holland or Germany, which may explain why the local name for the plum is the Dittisham Ploughman, a corruption of the German word 'pflaume' for plum. The Dittisham Plum season is very short, usually only lasting around 10 days. Nowadays much of the crop that is still grown in Dittisham is bought by the Bramley and Gage company in Bristol (www.bramleyandgage.co.uk) to make its Plum Liqueur.

Sheltered from the full force of the Atlantic westerlies by a narrow harbour entrance, and providing deep water anchorages for ships of up to 500ft, Dartmouth has a proud maritime history and is still a naval town – the imposing building overlooking the town in the background of this view is the Britannia Royal Naval College, the initial officer training establishment of the Royal Navy.

Dartmouth's 'New' Quay was built in 1585, on land reclaimed from tidal mud. Before that, ships tied up at the churchyard wall of St Saviour's Church which then overlooked the harbour. Consecrated in 1372, the church was enlarged and rebuilt in the 15th and 17th centuries. Its 15th-century rebuilding was undertaken by a famous character in Dartmouth's story, John Hawley (c1340-1408), who was buried in the chancel after his death – there is a fine memorial brass to him there. Hawley combined being a wealthy Dartmouth merchant, politican and fourteen times mayor of the town with another life as an adventurer, skilful mariner, privateer and raider of French ports during the Hundred Years War. It is often claimed that he was the inspiration for Geoffrey Chaucer's 'schipman' of 'Dertemouthe' in his 'Canterbury Tales', as Chaucer may have met Hawley when he visited the town as a customs officer in 1373; however, Chaucer may just have linked his colourful but nefarious seafaring character with Dartmouth because of the reputation the medieval town had for the general lawlessness of its seamen.

DARTMOUTH, THE TOWN AND RIVER 1931 84001

DARTMOUTH, THE QUAY AND HARBOUR c1955 D7027

Newcomen Road in Dartmouth is named after one of the town's most famous sons, Thomas Newcomen (c1663-1729), a local blacksmith and ironmonger. A serious problem of his times was water flooding coal and tin mines. Newcomen was keen to find a solution, as also was Thomas Savery (c1650-1715), a South Hams neighbour from Shilstone, near Modbury, who had patented a very crude steam engine to pump water out of mines, but which proved impractical for industrial use. Newcomen improved on Savery's design to develop an engine that worked purely by atmospheric pressure and created the first practical steam engine capable of raising water from deep mines, which was installed in a coal mine in 1712. Although they were very inefficient, mainly because the piston was open at the top, hundreds of Newcomen's steam engines were installed in British coal mines between then and 1775, when the Scottish engineer James Watt improved their efficiency by enclosing the piston. An original Newcomen engine, dating from about 1725 and still in working order, can be seen in The Newcomen Engine House next to the Tourist Information Centre in Dartmouth.

Dartmouth Castle was constructed in 1481 on a rocky promontory above the Dart next to St Petrock's Church, to guard the narrow entrance to the estuary and protect the prosperous town and its harbour against pirates and raiders. This was the first coastal fortress in England to be designed specifically for use by artillery, with a gun tower purpose-built to mount heavy cannon. Because of the limited range of cannon at that time, another castle was built on the opposite bank at Kingswear (seen in the background on the left of this view), so the estuary entrance could be protected from both sides. However, Kingwear Castle was abandoned within 50 years as gun technology improved, allowing the entire estuary to be protected by more powerful guns from Dartmouth Castle alone. The castle saw action during the Civil War, and continued in service right up until the Second World War. Successive updating of its defences included the Victorian Battery, which was built at the southern point of the main castle in the 1860s for five heavy guns positioned to protect the harbour entrance.

DARTMOUTH, BATTERY POINT 1889 21589

Start Bay runs from the mouth of the Dart estuary at the north down to the headland of Start Point in the south, with its lighthouse. Settlements along the coast of this large, sweeping bay are Stoke Fleming, Blackpool Sands, Strete, Slapton, Torcross, Beesands, and Hallsands. At Stoke Fleming, the 13th-century tower of the church of St Peter, on top of a hill, is a prominent landmark and was once used as a marker by ships entering the Dart estuary. Inside the church, the fine 14th-century memorial brass on the south side of the chancel step of John Corp (died 1390) and his granddaughter Eleyenore (died 1391) is the oldest to be found in any South Hams church.

Also of interest in Stoke Fleming's church is the wooden pulpit, which is decorated with a carved depiction of the Biblical story of Balaam and the ass as well as around 60 birds, insects and animals, including a spider on a cobweb. The carvings were done in 1891 by Violet Pinwill, who was only 17 years old at the time. Violet Pinwill was one of the daughters of the Reverend Edmund Pinwill, who became Vicar of Ermington, near Modbury, in 1880. Reverend Pinwill found Ermington's church in a bad state of disrepair, and Violet and her sisters Mary and Esther learned the art of woodcarving from the craftsmen he brought in to work on its restoration. The three sisters went on to form their own woodcarving business under the name of 'Rashleigh Pinwill' to repair and beautify Devon and Cornwall's medieval churches, specialising particularly in carvings of animals, flowers, fruits and vegetables; their work is sometimes found attributed to 'Mr R Pinwill'. Mary and Esther later left the business but Violet continued the work, employing and supervising a number of men and also executing the craft herself. There are examples of her work in over 100 churches. Violet Pinwill also worked in stone and created the magnificent alabaster of the Adoration of the baby Jesus in Ermington's church, where her craft first began.

The Start Bay area had a significant role during the Second World War in training for 'D-Day' in 1944. In November 1943 around 3,000 local people were told they had to evacuate the area by 20th December to allow American troops to rehearse for their role in the Normandy landings – Slapton Sands and its hinterland resembled 'Utah Beach' on the Cotentin peninsula, the destination of thousands of US soldiers who departed from local harbours such as Torquay, Dartmouth and Salcombe for the assault. They were to train under battle conditions, with live ammunition being extensively used in the rehearsals, including artillery bombardment, hence the need for local people to move away from the area between Strete and Torcross and inland as far as Blackawton and East Allington. An obelisk, a gift from the United States Army, now stands beside the beach at Slapton Sands, the inscription on its plaque thanking the people of the South Hams 'who generously left their homes and their lands to provide a battle practice area for the successful assault in Normandy in June 1944. Their action resulted in the saving of many hundreds of lives and contributed in no small measure to the success of the operation.'

Although the D-Day landings themselves were a success, the final rehearsal operation of 'Exercise Tiger' in April 1944 at Slapton Sands resulted in tragedy when 946 American soldiers lost their lives – many were killed when German E-boats intercepted the convoy of vessels travelling to Slapton from Portland for the exercise and sank three landing craft in Lyme Bay, and others died during the actual landings on the beach at Slapton when supporting naval vessels laid their artillery barrage too low. Details of the disaster were kept secret for many years but there are now several memorial plaques at Torcross to those who died, as well as a more unusual memorial in the shape of a Sherman amphibious tank that was lost during the exercise. It was recovered from the sea in the 1980s by a local man, Ken Small, who bought the tank as a sunken wreck from the American government for 50 dollars in 1974, salvaged and restored it, and installed it in the car park at Torcross as the first memorial there to the US servicemen who lost their lives.

At the southern end of Start Bay are Beesands and Hallsands. The Cricket Inn at Beesands has a place in musical history linked with Keith Richards and Mick Jagger of the Rolling Stones. Keith's family regularly holidayed at Beesands, and in the summer of 1961 his friend Mick Jagger joined them there for a while. Keith had taken his guitar on holiday with him, and it was at the Cricket Inn that he and Mick performed together for the first time in public.

Very little now remains of the original village of Hallsands. In the late 19th century the Admiralty started dredging 1,600 tons of shingle daily from just offshore to provide construction materials for the expansion of Devonport Dockyard near Plymouth. The dredging stopped in 1902 but the shingle never returned, leaving the village without its natural protection against the power of the sea in winter storms, and it suffered a number of floods over the years. Then in January 1917 a combination of easterly gales and exceptionally high tides destroyed the village when part of the cliff above Hallsands gave way. Most of Hallsands was washed into the sea, and its inhabitants had to move to new homes built further inland.

Start Point, at the southern end of Start Bay, is one of the most exposed peninsulas around the south-west coast of England, running out to sea for almost a mile. Since 1836 it has been guarded by the Start Point lighthouse, designed by James Walker as a 92ft-high circular castellated tower. The Start Point light was automated in 1993, when the last lighthouse-keepers left the tower.

Further west along the coast from Start Point is Prawle Point, the southernmost point of Devon. Because of its position it has served as a lookout since ancient times – the name 'Prawle' probably derives from the Old English 'Præwhyll', meaning a 'look-out', or 'look-out hill'.

TORBAY & THE SOUTH HAMS
A MISCELLANY

Salcombe, Devon's most southerly town, lies at the mouth of the Kingsbridge estuary, although this is actually a ria, or drowned valley that was inundated by rising sea levels, with no major river flowing into it. The sheltered tidal estuary is an area of special scientific interest, where a variety of habitats such as reed beds and mud flats support some unusual and often rare species of seaweed, plant or animal. Amongst the creatures found there are seahorses, which inhabit the eelgrass beds along the lower fringe of the foreshore.

A few ruined walls on a rocky outcrop beside the estuary mark the site of Fort Charles, otherwise known as Salcombe Castle, which was garrisoned by a Royalist force from January to May 1646 during the closing stages of the English Civil War, and was the last place to hold out in the Royalist cause against the victorious Parliamentarians. So bravely did the Royalists defend this hopeless position that the Parliamentarian commander allowed them to leave with colours flying after they surrendered when it was clear their cause was lost. After the war the castle was deliberately ruined by order of Parliament to prevent it being of further military use.

SALCOMBE, FROM PORTLEMOUTH 1928 81014

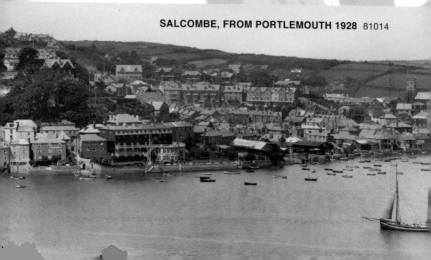

In the 18th and 19th centuries Salcombe was a centre of boat and shipbuilding, and was especially famous for the 'Salcombe fruiters' built there. These sleek, clipper-like schooners traded commodities such as oranges, lemons and pineapples, tobacco, coffee, ginger, sugar, rum, coconuts and cotton from the Azores, Bahamas, Mediterranean and West Indies as well as wood such as ebony and mahogany. They were specifically built for speed, so they could race back as fast as possible with their valuable but perishable cargo. Salcombe's Maritime Museum holds a fine collection of accurately detailed portraits of 19th-century Salcombe-built sailing ships, many of which were painted in a foreign port by a 'pierhead artist' commissioned by the ship's proud captain.

The Maritime Museum also holds sadder relics in its Wreck Room, a collection of items recovered by divers from the many shipwrecks that have occurred off this dangerous part of the South Devon coast. Amongs these are tin ingots from a Bronze Age trading vessel that sank off Prawle Point between 1200 and 900BC. Although nothing remains of the boat's structure, many items have been recovered from the wreck site since it was discovered. These include weapons, jewellery and a large cargo of copper and tin ingots. The finds originate from several sources in Europe, showing that this part of Bronze Age Britain was part of a European-wide trade network dealing in commodities of the time.

The Wreck Room of the Maritime Museum also holds artifacts recovered from HMS 'Ramillies', a 90-gun ship of the line of the Royal Navy which sank in 1760 off the headland of Bolt Tail, west of Salcombe. After leaving Plymouth she had headed into a massive south-westerly gale and been blown around the Channel for 9 days. She was wrecked on the cliffs below Bolt Tail as she tried to return to the safety of Plymouth, with the loss of 708 of her 734 crew. The tragedy is commemorated in the name of Ramillies Cove, a short distance east of the tip of Bolt Tail.

Kingsbridge lies at the head of the Kingsbridge estuary, so named because the first bridge there linked two royal estates at Alvington and Chillington and was called 'the king's bridge'. It was once an important inland port with quays built over the mudflats on the shoreline of Kingsbridge Creek, importing timber, barley, livestock and building materials, and exporting corn, slate and locally produced malt and cider. The end of the creek seen in this view has now been filled in and the area is a parking space for buses and taxis, and the gabled building left of centre now houses a Boots store.

Duncombe Street in Kingsbridge is named after William Duncombe who was the first headmaster of the grammar school founded in the 17th century by Thomas Crispin, a wealthy fuller in the wool trade. The old grammar school building in Fore Street now houses the Cookworthy Museum, named after William Cookworthy, born in Kingsbridge in 1705, who can be credited as the father of the china clay industry in Devon and Cornwall. It was Cookworthy who, in 1746, discovered the first deposits of china clay in Cornwall, and devised a way of making the first true hard-paste English porcelain with it. He patented his methods and founded a porcelain factory at Plymouth in 1768.

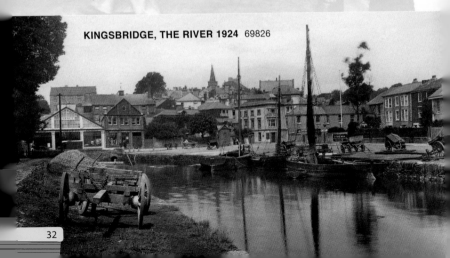

KINGSBRIDGE, THE RIVER 1924 69826

KINGSBRIDGE, FORE STREET 1896 38429

The clock tower seen in the distance of this view of Fore Street
surmounts what was once Kingbridge's Town Hall, although the
building is now used for other purposes. There are clock-faces on
three of the four sides of its grandiose clock, but the fourth side is
blank – the local legend is that this is because when the clock was
erected on the Town Hall in 1875 this side of it could be seen from
the workhouse, and the authorities did not want its inmates clock-
watching whilst they worked! Also seen in the background of this
view is St Edmund's Church, famous for the epitaph on the chancel
door to Robert Phillip who died in 1793 and 'at whose request the
following lines are here inserted':

> 'Here lie I at the chancel door,
> Here lie I because I'm poor,
> The further in, the more you pay,
> Here lie I as warm as they.'

33

The River Avon flows down through the South Hams from its source on Dartmoor to empty into Bigbury Bay. The first major settlement it reaches is South Brent, which was once a woollen and market centre. The building with the bellcote on the roof on the right of this view is the old Toll House, where market tolls were paid. It is now an information centre where you can still see the tariff board (dated 1889) displaying the various tolls charged for the goods brought to market – for example, a cart bringing fish was charged 2 shillings and 6 pence, whilst a cart drawn by one donkey was only charged 1 penny.

Although they have been widened and altered since they were first built, two narrow packhorse bridges cross the river about half a mile north and south of the village centre. Packhorses were the usual bulk carriers in inland Devon for centuries, transporting all manner of goods in panniers mounted on wooden frames. The packhorse trains that passed through South Brent in the past are recelled in the name of the Pack Horse Inn in Plymouth Road, which was once a packhorse station on the Plymouth to London road.

SOUTH BRENT, CHURCH STREET c1955 S360003

From South Brent the Avon flows past Avonwick, where the little church of St James is a 'proprietary chapel', an Anglican place of worship built and maintained by a private person or founders – the building of Avonwick's church was organised and paid for by local worthies Mr and Mrs Cornish-Bowden, and completed in 1878. Proprietary chapels are anomalies in English ecclesiastical law, having no parish area but licenced for divine services to be performed there by a member of the clergy according to the rites of the Church of England. Before Avonwick had its own church the villagers had to travel some distance to worship at either of four churches in the area, one of which was Ugborough, whose large church of St Peter is famous for the fine series of 14th-century carved wooden bosses on the timber roof of its north aisle. One represents St Eloy, the patron saint of metal workers and goldsmiths, as a smith with his anvil, and another shows a sow with her litter of eight piglets, representing the legend of St Brannock, a 6th-century Welsh abbot who came to Devon on a missionary journey. He dreamed that he should build a church where he found a white sow and eight piglets, which he did at Braunton in North Devon.

Further south, the Avon valley is overlooked by Blackdown Rings, an Iron Age banked enclosure with the earthwork remains of an early medieval motte and bailey castle on Blackdown Hill. From the hilltop there is a panoramic view looking southwards across the South Hams. Access to Blackdown Rings is signposted off the B3196 north of Loddiswell. Further along this road, east of Brownston, is the area known as California Cross. This used to be known as Brownston Cross, but was probably renamed because this point on the road was the last stop for coaches carrying passengers to Plymouth to embark for America during the California gold rush of the 1840s and 50s. However, those hopeful goldpanners might have done better to have stayed in Devon and looked for gold there instead – panned samples of alluvial grains collected south of a line from Plymouth to Brixham have shown that gold is widely distributed over much of the South Hams area, and also present in carbonate veins on the promontory headland of Hope's Nose, east of Torquay. Yes siree, there's gold in them thar hills!

Loddiswell's most famous son was Richard Peek, born there in 1782. He became known as 'Little Dick Whittington' because as a young man he walked from Devon to London where he made his fortune as a tea broker and was Sherriff of London from 1832-33. He then retired to Loddiswell where he had built himself a grand home, Hazelwood House (now a hotel). He was a great local benefactor and also a prominent abolitionist, and appears in the painting by Benjamin Robert Haydon of those attending The Anti-Slavery Society Convention in London in 1840 that hangs in the National Portrait Gallery.

From Aveton Gifford the Avon winds through its tidal estuary to Bigbury Bay. On its eastern bank before the river meets the sea is Bantham, where the Sloop Inn was once owned by Nat Cleverley, a notorious smuggler of rum, brandy and other illicit goods. Cleverley was eventually caught by the Revenue men and brought to trial, but found 'not guilty' – probably because the magistrate who tried him was one of his best customers!

Thurlestone lies on the coast of Bigbury Bay east of the mouth of the Avon. It takes its name from the offshore pinnacle of Thurlestone Rock, an imposing stone arch which has been holed, or 'thurled', by the sea. The arch is a made of New Red Sandstone, a rock so hard that it has remained standing whilst all the other rocks around it have been washed away by the violence of the waves, giving rise to the old Devon saying:

'Brave every shock
Like Thurlestone Rock.'

THURLESTONE, THE ROCK
1925 78316

BIGBURY-ON-SEA, THE BURGH ISLAND HOTEL AND TRACTOR 1931 83969X

Just off the mainland at Bigbury-on-Sea is Burgh Island. It is possible to walk out to the island at low water, when it is linked to the mainland by a broad spit of land, but when the tide is in visitors are ferried across by the famous Burgh Island Sea Tractor. The machine making its way through the surf in this 1930s view no longer exists, but the current version (designed in 1969) serves the same purpose and is the only hydraulic Sea Tractor in the world.

The Burgh Island Hotel was built in 1929 and is one of England's finest surviving Art Deco hotels. It is now restored to its 1930s' glamour, recalling the days when it was a favourite haunt of the rich, famous and fashionable, including Agatha Christie. Whilst staying in the hotel she wrote part of 'And Then There Were None' and her Hercule Poirot mystery 'Evil Under the Sun', in which she based the Jolly Roger Hotel on the Burgh Island Hotel – which appears as such in the 2001 TV adaption of the novel, starring David Suchet as the moustachioed Belgian detective, that was filmed on the island.

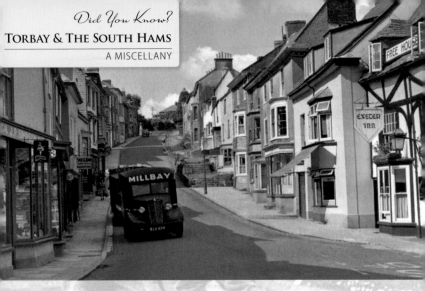

MODBURY, CHURCH STREET c1955 M172014

Modbury became very wealthy in the 18th and early 19th centuries from the making of woollen serge cloth. Its cloth trade and its prosperity declined in the 1800s with the rise of the Yorkshire woollen industry, but Modbury remained an important stopping off place for stage coach travellers, with many inns. One was the Exeter Inn in Church Street, which dates from the 14th century and is the oldest surviving inn in the town.

Modbury was the site of two battles in the Civil War. The first was on December 9th 1642, when a small Royalist force saw off a smaller force of Parliamentarians. The second was a more serious affair that raged for twelve hours on February 21st 1643, when around 2,000 Royalists defending Modbury were attacked by around 8,000 Parliamentarians in fields outside the town on the eastern side – the site is now marked with a plaque in Galpin Street. The Royalists were driven back into Modbury before eventually retreating out of the town and away to the west along the footpath that leads off Church Lane behind St George's Church – hence its name of Runaway Lane.

The bells of Modbury's impressive 13th-century St George's Church are reputed to be among the top ten of Devon and an old rhyme proudly boasts about their pre-eminence over those of the town's near neighbour of Ermington across the River Erme:

> *'Hark to Modbury bells*
> *How they do quiver*
> *Better than Ermington bells*
> *Down by the river.'*

Ermington's church may not be famous for its bells, but it certainly is for its crooked spire. The spire probably twisted because the timbers used in its construction in the 14th century were not properly seasoned and the structure warped over the years, exacerbated by the weight of the stone that covered it. However, a much more romantic reason is the local legend that one of the first brides to be married in the church was so beautiful that the spire leaned round and bowed to her. The spire was rebuilt in the 1850s but the shape of its twist was retained, at the request of the villagers.

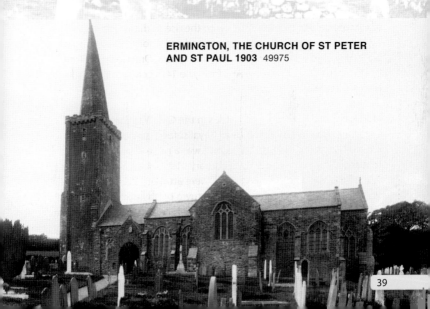

ERMINGTON, THE CHURCH OF ST PETER AND ST PAUL 1903 49975

The largest town of the South Hams is Ivybridge, where the River Erme surges under the narrow ancient bridge that gave the town its name. The bridge was widened in the 18th century when the road from South Brent to Plymouth was turnpiked and the age of the mail and stage coach began. However, coaches found it hard to negotiate the double bend around the old bridge as they approached the London Hotel (a former coaching inn now converted into flats called London Court), so a new bridge was built in the early 19th century, connecting Fore Street and Exeter Road.

Before Ivybridge became a civil parish in its own right in 1894 it was part of four neighbouring parishes, of Harford, Ugborough, Ermington and Cornwood. All four parish boundaries met at the old bridge and were marked with stones at each of its corners, two of which still survive on the bridge. Another feature of the bridge is the iron stave set into its lip, which in past times was filled with wood that was lit at night to burn and illuminate the highway – an early form of street lighting!

IVYBRIDGE, THE OLD BRIDGE AND THE LONDON HOTEL c1955 I22032

IVYBRIDGE, ALLEN'S PAPER MILLS c1876 8310

The purity of the water of the River Erme as it flows through granite off Dartmoor makes it ideal for papermaking, and it played a part in the making of paper at Ivybridge for around 200 years. The papermill seen in this view is Stowford Mill in Harford Road, seen here c1876 when it was owned by John Allen who was a great benefactor to the town – in 1874 he funded the construction of the present Methodist Church in Fore Street, and he built a number of homes for his employees around the town, including the ten dwellings in Fore Street known as Allen's Cottages. The oldest part of the mill dates from the mid 19th century, but it was badly damaged by fire in 1914 and largely rebuilt. At one time the mill produced paper for the old white five pound notes and for stamps, and in more recent years the Stowford Paper Mill has been operated by ArjoWiggins (Ivybridge) Ltd, manufacturing high quality speciality security, printing and writing paper. Sadly, papermaking in Ivybridge will come to an end in 2014 when ArjoWiggins closes Stowford Paper Mill and transfers its operations to Aberdeen in Scotland.

A major landmark of Ivybridge is the railway viaduct over the River Erme. The original viaduct was built by Isambard Kingdom Brunel in 1848 for the South Devon Railway on granite piers with an upper superstructure of timber. One the most beautiful of Brunel's wooden viaducts, the elegant structure was described in 'Murray's Handbook for Devon and Cornwall' of 1859 as 'a spider-like fabric of such slender proportions that one wonders it has not been blown away into the moor... a black wooden roadway, which is carried in a curve over ten pairs of white granite pillars, each pair being sixty feet apart, and the most elevated a hundred and fifteen feet above the valley.' Brunel's viaduct was replaced in the 1890s with the impressive stone structure that now carries main line trains connecting London and Penzance across the Erme valley, but remnants of the granite piers of the earlier viaduct can still be seen standing alongside it in Longtimber Woods, off Station Road. Brunel's original timber viaduct can be seen in the background of this view from 1890, shortly before it was replaced with the current structure.

IVYBRIDGE, GENERAL VIEW 1890 22517

42

North of Ivybridge on the River Erme is Harford, where the river flows under its first road bridge since rising at Erme Head on Dartmoor. St Petroc's Church at Harford contains the tomb chest of Thomas Williams, who was Speaker of the House of Commons from 1563 until his death in 1566, during the reign of Queen Elizabeth I. His family home was Stowford House near Ivybridge, the former manor house for Harford, where he was born c1514. On top of his tomb is an interesting memorial brass of him wearing a full set of armour.

Standing in Harford's churchyard is an old granite cross that was once a waymarker on the Abbot's Way, the ancient track that skirts the southern edge of Dartmoor and in medieval times was a route between Buckfast Abbey and Plympton Priory. In 1909 the cross was discovered in Harford Moor Lane, where it was being used as a gatepost, and it was moved into the churchyard for safekeeping. It is thought that the cross originally stood not far from where it was found in its gatepost role, where it guided walkers from the moor to the village lane.

On the eastern side of the Erme a mile upstream from Harford is Piles Copse (OS Grid Reference SX644620), a woodland of stunted and contorted pedunculate oak trees which is one of the last three remnants of the ancient forest that once covered much of Dartmoor – the other two are Wistman's Wood near Two Bridges and Black Tor Copse in the north of the moor. These three sites on Dartmoor make up three of only five remnants of high altitude oak woodlands that still survive in Britain – the other two are both in Cumbria – and which are believed to be relics of primeval woodland that survived the original clearance of the uplands by prehistoric man. The trunks and branches of the gnarled, ancient trees are covered with lichens and mosses, some of which are rare.

From its source on Dartmoor, the River Plym flows along part of the northern boundary of the South Hams before converging with the Meavy just upstream of Shaugh Bridge, near Shaugh Prior. China clay extraction has been a feature of this part of south Dartmoor since the mid 19th century, and the clay used to be brought to Shaugh Bridge by pipe in slurry form and dried out there before being transferred away. The remains of the old clay drying kilns and loading bays can still be seen there, where they form one side of the car park for access into the surrounding woodland.

From Shaugh Bridge the Plym flows south to empty into the sea west of Plympton. Although both Plympton and Plymstock, further south, are historically and geographically part of the South Hams area, they have officially been part of the City of Plymouth since 1967.

Between Plymouth South and the Yealm estuary is the Wembury Peninsula, with its seaside resorts of Heybrook Bay and Wembury. Offshore is the Great Mew Stone, a small uninhabited island which is now a bird sanctuary and closed to visitors, although in the past it has been both a prison and a private home. In 1744 a local man was sentenced to be 'transported' to the island, where he lived with his family for seven years. His daughter, known as 'Black Joan', chose to remain there after the sentence was served, and is said to have acted as a lookout for the Devon smuggler Jack Rattenbury. The last people to live there were Sam Wakeham and his wife Ann, who married in 1833 in Wembury's church and lived in a quaint turreted dwelling Sam built on the island. At that time the island was a rabbit warren for the Langdon Estate, and the Wakehams lived there rent free in return for Sam protecting the rabbits from poachers; he also made a few pence by rowing people across to the island for visits. Unfortunately Sam was also a smuggler, and he and his family had to leave the Great Mew Stone when his actitivies were discovered, and he became a boatman in Plymouth.

Yealmpton (pronounced 'Yampton') stands on the River Yealm near the end of its journey from Dartmoor to the sea. Most of its parish church dates from 1849-52 when the nave and chancel of the medieval church were rebuilt to designs of William Butterfield, but the crumbling tower of the earlier church was not replaced until 1915. The cost of rebuilding the tower was met with thousands of donations after the vicar of the time wrote a letter to children under the name of the nursery rhyme character 'Old Mother Hubbard', which was reprinted all over the world. He did this because of the link between Yealmpton and the rhyme, which was written in 1804 by Sarah Martin as an entertainment whilst she was staying at nearby Kitley House, the home of her sister Judith and her husband, John Polloxfen Bastard. There is a local tradition that Mother Hubbard was based on the housekeeper of Kitley House at the time of Miss Martin's visit, who later retired to an old thatched cottage in Market Street, opposite the Rose & Crown pub – seen in the photograph on the Contents page of this book.

YEALMPTON, FROM THE BRIDGE 1904 52428

SPORTING TORBAY
& THE SOUTH HAMS

Sailing regattas take place in many places around the area. Many of them feature events for boats that were developed from the local fishing industry, such as the Salcombe Yawls, racing dinghies that originated from small fishing boats which had to be capable of sailing to windward in strong tides to work crab and lobster pots. One of the biggest events is the Port of Dartmouth Royal Regatta. This photograph shows what the Dartmouth Regatta looked like in the past, when 'The Line' was one of its grand sights – large yachts moored on the trots to form an honour guard for rowing crews.

The golf course at Thurlestone was started in 1897 and is one of the most beautiful courses in the south-west, enjoying a spectacular setting high above the coastline of Bigbury Bay. In 1974 Harry Pratt became world-famous when he scored a hole in one at the sixth, when he was aged just seven!

The Totnes Orange Races take place in August each year, when contestants chase oranges down the steep High Street and Fore Street of the town, kicking or throwing the fruit as they go. The Orange Races are supposed to commemorate a visit to Totnes of that old Elizabethan seadog and famous son of Devon, Sir Francis Drake; apparently he knocked over a basket of oranges and the townspeople chased after them as they hurtled down the hill, trying to retrieve the fruit.

Torquay United Football Club's nickname is 'The Gulls'. Possibly their finest hour was in the FA Cup tournament of the 1954/55 season, when they held Leeds United to a 2-2 draw – and then beat them 4-0 on the replay to reach the fourth round – where sadly, their running streak came to an end against Huddersfield Town. Another notable victory in the club's history was in 1991, when The Gulls defeated Blackpool on penalties at Wembley in the Fourth Division play-off final to win promotion to the Third Division – earning a place in sporting history as the first Football League team to win promotion on penalties.

The small village of Avonwick, near South Brent, is the home of one of the oldest lawn tennis clubs in the world. The Avon Vale Tennis and Croquet Club was originally founded in 1859 as an archery club, then other sports were introduced, including tennis, and the club held its first tennis tournament in 1879. It is believed to be the third oldest club in the world still playing on its original tennis courts.

A famous name in British tennis is Sue Barker, now a BBC sports commentator, who was born in Paignton in 1956. During her playing career she was ranked British Number 1, and at her peak was ranked World Number 3; she also reached the semi-final of the women's singles tournament at Wimbledon in 1977.

DARTMOUTH, THE REGATTA 1886 21652

QUIZ QUESTIONS

Answers on page 52.

1. Building a community under the rocky cliffs of Brixham led to many unusually-shaped buildings designed to fit into the odd corners of the steep and winding streets. A famous example is the Coffin House at the junction of Temperance Place and King Street, seen in the photograph on the opposite page in 1904, when it was being used as a barber's shop. What is the romantic legend linked with this building?

2. Which popular TV comedy series was inspired by a visit to Torquay in 1970?

3. Most famous for her crime novels, the Torquay-born authoress Agatha Christie also wrote six romantic novels under a pseudonym – what was it?

4. What unusual event takes place each year at the South Hams village of Blackawton, west of Dartmouth?

5. In Devon dialect, what does it mean if something is 'crumpety'?

6. Which South Hams village holds its own version of Whacky Races?

7. What and where was 'The Primrose Line'?

8. What is the link between the South Hams town of Modbury and cowboy hats?

9. The rugged coastal area around the headland of Prawle Point, south-west of Salcombe, is one of the few places in the UK where you can see a rare bird whose Latin name is 'Emberiza cirlus' – by what name is it better known?

10. Whereabouts in the Torbay and South Hams area might you find Orange Elephants? (And the answer is NOT at Paignton Zoo!)

BRIXHAM, THE COFFIN HOUSE
1904 53146x

YE Olde Coffin House
ONLY ONE IN ENGLAND

YE OLDE
COFFIN HOUSE
SHAVING SALOON

V.CROCKER

RECIPE

Torbay Sole with Lemon and Caper Sauce

Torbay is famous for its sole, which is at its best from July to February.
Torbay sole is also known as lemon sole, and witch sole is also caught,
similar to lemon sole but thinner. In this recipe, fillets of Torbay sole
are served with a zesty dressing that is also good with skate, plaice,
brill and Dover sole. Serves 4.

4 large or 8 small fillets of Torbay (lemon) sole,
  with the black skin removed
2 tablespoonfuls plain flour
25g/1oz butter, melted
Salt and pepper
For the dressing:
Juice of 2 lemons
50g/2oz unsalted butter
4 teaspoonfuls capers, drained and rinsed
1 tablespoonful chopped fresh parsley

Pre-heat the grill to hot. Line a grill pan with kitchen foil and place
it under the grill to heat up. Toss the fish fillets in the flour so that all
sides are lightly coated, then brush both sides of the fish with the
melted butter and season to taste with salt and pepper. Place the
fish fillets on the hot foil in the grill pan. Cook under a hot grill for 2-8
minutes depending on the thickness of the fish fillets, without turning
them over, until they are golden brown. When cooked, arrange the fish
on a hot serving dish, and keep warm whilst you make the dressing.

Add 4 tablespoonfuls of water to the lemon juice. Heat the butter in
a heavy-based pan until it is melted and browned, but not scorched.
Add the lemon juice, half at first, then taste the sauce and add the
other half if you want. Add the capers and parsley, and season well to
taste. Pour the dressing over the fish and serve, with vegetables such
as new potatoes and peas, green beans or wilted spinach.

RECIPE

Dartmouth Pie (or Devon Pork Pie)

6 pork chops, boned, trimmed of fat and cut in half
  if very large
(or 675g/1½ lbs leg of pork, cut into thin slices)
6 medium-sized leeks, trimmed and sliced, or 3 onions,
  peeled and thinly sliced
3 large cooking apples, peeled, cored and cut
  into slices
2 tablespoonfuls soft brown sugar
Half a teaspoonful freshly grated nutmeg
Half a teaspoonful ground allspice
300ml/ ½ pint dry cider or good stock
225g/8oz shortcrust pastry
Beaten egg or milk to glaze the pastry
Salt and pepper

Pre-heat the oven to 200°C/400°F/Gas Mark 6 and grease a deep
pie dish. Place half the meat in the dish, followed by a layer of
apples. Sprinkle over half the sugar and spices, then add a layer
of leeks or onions. Season well with salt and pepper. Repeat the
layers with the remaining ingredients, then pour in the cider or
stock. Roll out the pastry to 2cms (¾ inch) larger than the top of
the pie dish. Cut a narrow strip from around the pastry, dampen
the rim of the dish and fit the strip around it. Brush the strip with
water, then lay the pastry lid over the dish, pressing the edges
together well to seal them. Brush the lid with beaten egg or milk,
and cut two holes in the centre to allow steam to escape. Bake in
the pre-heated oven for 20 minutes, then reduce the temperature
to 170°C/325°F/ Gas Mark 3, cover the pie with foil, and continue
to cook for 1-1¼ hours.

QUIZ ANSWERS

1. The story goes that a young couple of the town wanted to marry, but the girl's father declared he would rather see her in a coffin than allow her to wed the man of her choice. Undeterred, her suitor built (or bought) the narrow, coffin-shaped property, named it the Coffin House and claimed his bride, telling his future father-in-law that his wish would be met! The girl's father was so impressed that he gave his consent to the marriage.

2. 'Fawlty Towers'. In 1970 the 'Monty Python's Flying Circus' team were staying at the Gleneagles Hotel in Torquay whilst filming for their television series. According to the Monty Python member John Cleese, the proprietor of the hotel was 'the most wonderfully rude man I have ever met' and inspired his Basil Fawlty character, the incredibly rude and wayward proprietor of a fictional hotel called 'Fawlty Towers'.

3. Agatha Christie wrote six romantic novels under the pseudonym of Mary Westmacott: 'Absent in the Spring', 'The Burden', 'Unfinished Portrait', 'A Daughter's A Daughter', 'The Rose and the Yew Tree' and 'Giant's Bread'.

4. Blackawton hosts a Worm Charming Festival every year, which takes place on the May Day Bank Holiday in a field near the village. Worm charming is an eccentric activity that originated as a way of collecting bait for fishing, but has developed into a competitive sport. It involves vibrating the soil in some way to encourage worms to come to the surface, and contestants tap or dance on the ground to bring as many worms as possible up to the surface of their allotted one-metre-square patch of soil. A further bizarre touch is added to the festival by many of the competitors wearing fancy dress.

5. 'Crumpetty' means twisted or crooked – just like the crumpetty spire of the church at Ermington!

6. East Allington, near Kingsbridge. Every May the road through the village is closed for the Whacky Races, when home-made go-karts race downhill against the clock along a course lined with hay bales and crowds of people. Go-karters come from all over the country to take part and 'challenge the cream of East Allington racers', to quote from the event's website: www.eastallingtonwhackyraces.co.uk.

7. 'The Primrose Line' was a single track railway line of the South Hams that ran between Brent Station, just outside South Brent, and Kingsbridge, much of its route passing through the valley of the River Avon. It was a branch line of the Great Western Railway that opened in 1893 and ran until 1963 when it was closed. It was reckoned to be the most beautiful line in the country, and was known as the 'Primrose Line' because of the spring flowers which lined its route.

8. The John B Stetson Company in the USA was founded by the hat manufacturer John Batterson Stetson (1830-1906), credited as the inventor in the 1860s of the cowboy hat, commonly referred to as a 'Stetson'. John B Stetson was descended from Modbury native Robert Stetson and his first wife Honour Tucker, who married in St Andrew's Church at Plymouth and emigrated to Massachusetts around 1634.

9. 'Emberiza cirlus' is the Latin name for the rare Cirl Bunting, a relative of the Yellowhammer with yellowish-green body plumage with red-brown patches, and a striking yellow-striped head. Prawle Point is one of the best places to see this charming and pretty bird, but it is also present on a number of nature reserves in the South Hams.

10. You might find 'Orange Elephants' grazing in the fields around the area – that is the nickname for South Devon cattle, which are orangy-brown in colour and the largest of the British native cattle breeds.

FRANCIS FRITH

PIONEER   VICTORIAN   PHOTOGRAPHER

Francis Frith, founder of the world-famous photographic archive, was a complex and multi-talented man. A devout Quaker and a highly successful Victorian businessman, he was philosophical by nature and pioneering in outlook. By 1855 he had already established a wholesale grocery business in Liverpool, and sold it for the astonishing sum of £200,000, which is the equivalent today of over £15,000,000. Now in his thirties, and captivated by the new science of photography, Frith set out on a series of pioneering journeys up the Nile and to the Near East.

INTRIGUE AND EXPLORATION

He was the first photographer to venture beyond the sixth cataract of the Nile. Africa was still the mysterious 'Dark Continent', and Stanley and Livingstone's historic meeting was a decade into the future. The conditions for picture taking confound belief. He laboured for hours in his wicker dark-room in the sweltering heat of the desert, while the volatile chemicals fizzed dangerously in their trays. Back in London he exhibited his photographs and was 'rapturously cheered' by members of the Royal Society. His reputation as a photographer was made overnight.

VENTURE OF A LIFE-TIME

By the 1870s the railways had threaded their way across the country, and Bank Holidays and half-day Saturdays had been made obligatory by Act of Parliament. All of a sudden the working man and his family were able to enjoy days out, take holidays, and see a little more of the world.

With typical business acumen, Francis Frith foresaw that these new tourists would enjoy having souvenirs to commemorate their days out. For the next thirty years he travelled the country by train and by pony and trap, producing fine photographs of seaside resorts and beauty spots that were keenly bought by millions of Victorians. These prints were painstakingly pasted into family albums and pored over during the dark nights of winter, rekindling precious memories of summer excursions. Frith's studio was soon supplying retail shops all over the country, and by 1890 F Frith & Co had become the greatest specialist photographic publishing company in the world, with over 2,000 sales outlets, and pioneered the picture postcard.

FRANCIS FRITH'S LEGACY

Francis Frith had died in 1898 at his villa in Cannes, his great project still growing. By 1970 the archive he created contained over a third of a million pictures showing 7,000 British towns and villages.

Frith's legacy to us today is of immense significance and value, for the magnificent archive of evocative photographs he created provides a unique record of change in the cities, towns and villages throughout Britain over a century and more. Frith and his fellow studio photographers revisited locations many times down the years to update their views, compiling for us an enthralling and colourful pageant of British life and character.

We are fortunate that Frith was dedicated to recording the minutiae of everyday life. For it is this sheer wealth of visual data, the painstaking chronicle of changes in dress, transport, street layouts, buildings, housing and landscape that captivates us so much today, offering us a powerful link with the past and with the lives of our ancestors.

Computers have now made it possible for Frith's many thousands of images to be accessed almost instantly. The archive offers every one of us an opportunity to examine the places where we and our families have lived and worked down the years. Its images, depicting our shared past, are now bringing pleasure and enlightenment to millions around the world a century and more after his death.

For further information visit: www.francisfrith.com

INTERIOR DECORATION

Frith's photographs can be seen framed and as giant wall murals in thousands of pubs, restaurants, hotels, banks, retail stores and other public buildings throughout Britain. These provide interesting and attractive décor, generating strong local interest and acting as a powerful reminder of gentler days in our increasingly busy and frenetic world.

FRITH PRODUCTS

All Frith photographs are available as prints and posters in a variety of different sizes and styles. In the UK we also offer a range of other gift and stationery products illustrated with Frith photographs, although many of these are not available for delivery outside the UK – see our web site for more information on the products available for delivery in your country.

THE INTERNET

Over 100,000 photographs of Britain can be viewed and purchased on the Frith web site. The web site also includes memories and reminiscences contributed by our customers, who have personal knowledge of localities and of the people and properties depicted in Frith photographs. If you wish to learn more about a specific town or village you may find these reminiscences fascinating to browse. Why not add your own comments if you think they would be of interest to others? See **www.francisfrith.com**

PLEASE HELP US BRING FRITH'S PHOTOGRAPHS TO LIFE

Our authors do their best to recount the history of the places they write about. They give insights into how particular towns and villages developed, they describe the architecture of streets and buildings, and they discuss the lives of famous people who lived there. But however knowledgeable our authors are, the story they tell is necessarily incomplete.

Frith's photographs are so much more than plain historical documents. They are living proofs of the flow of human life down the generations. They show real people at real moments in history; and each of those people is the son or daughter of someone, the brother or sister, aunt or uncle, grandfather or grandmother of someone else. All of them lived, worked and played in the streets depicted in Frith's photographs.

We would be grateful if you would give us your insights into the places shown in our photographs: the streets and buildings, the shops, businesses and industries. Post your memories of life in those streets on the Frith website: what it was like growing up there, who ran the local shop and what shopping was like years ago; if your workplace is shown tell us about your working day and what the building is used for now. Read other visitors' memories and reconnect with your shared local history and heritage. With your help more and more Frith photographs can be brought to life, and vital memories preserved for posterity, and for the benefit of historians in the future.

Wherever possible, we will try to include some of your comments in future editions of our books. Moreover, if you spot errors in dates, titles or other facts, please let us know, because our archive records are not always completely accurate—they rely on 140 years of human endeavour and hand-compiled records. You can email us using the contact form on the website.

Thank you!

For further information, trade, or author enquiries
please contact us at the address below:

**The Francis Frith Collection, 6 Oakley Business Park,
Wylye Road, Dinton, Salisbury, Wiltshire, England SP3 5EUv.**
Tel: +44 (0)1722 716 376 Fax: +44 (0)1722 716 881
e-mail: sales@francisfrith.co.uk **www.francisfrith.com**